JOANNA MURRAY-SMITH's plays have been produced throughout Australia and all over the world, including *Honour*, which had a public reading with Meryl Streep and was produced on Broadway in 1998, the National Theatre, London, in 2003, and on the West End with Dame Diana Rigg in 2005. Other plays include *Berlin*; *Three Little Words*; *L'Appartement*; *Fury*; *Songs for Nobodies*; *Switzerland*; *Pennsylvania Avenue*; *True Minds*; *Day One, A Hotel, Evening*; *Rockabye*; *Ninety*; *Bombshells*; *Rapture*; *Nightfall*; *Redemption*; *Love Child*; *Atlanta*; *Flame* and acclaimed adaptations of *Hedda Gabler* and *Scenes from a Marriage*, many of which have been translated into other languages. She has been nominated for and won many awards.

Jessica Bentley and Justine Clarke in JULIA, 2023, co-produced by Sydney Theatre Company and Canberra Theatre Centre. (Photo © Prudence Upton)

JULIA

JOANNA MURRAY-SMITH

CURRENCY PRESS
The performing arts publisher

CURRENCY PLAYS

First published in 2023
by Currency Press
Gadigal Land, PO Box 2287 Strawberry Hills, NSW, 2012, Australia
enquiries@currency.com.au
www.currency.com.au

Introduction: The clocks, the bells copyright © Charlotte Wood, 2023; *Julia* copyright © Tropolis Pty Ltd, 2023.

COPYING FOR EDUCATIONAL PURPOSES

The Australian *Copyright Act 1968* [Act] allows a maximum of one chapter or 10% of this book, whichever is the greater, to be copied by any educational institution for its educational purposes provided that that educational institution [or the body that administers it] has given a remuneration notice to Copyright Agency [CA] under the Act.

For details of the CA licence for educational institutions contact CA,
12 / 66 Goulburn Street, Sydney, NSW, 2000; tel: within Australia 1800 066 844 toll free; outside Australia 61 2 9394 7600; fax: 61 2 9394 7601;
email: memberservices@copyright.com.au

COPYING FOR OTHER PURPOSES

Except as permitted under the Act, for example a fair dealing for the purposes of study, research, criticism or review, no part of this book may be reproduced, stored in a retrieval system, or transmitted in any form or by any means without prior written permission. All enquiries should be made to the publisher at the address above.
Any performance or public reading of *Julia* is forbidden unless a licence has been received from the author or the author's agent. The purchase of this book in no way gives the purchaser the right to perform the play in public, whether by means of a staged production or a reading. All applications for public performance should be addressed to the author c/- Currency Press.

Six Bells by Gillian Clarke is reprinted by kind permission of Carcanet Press, Manchester, UK.

Typeset by Brighton Gray for Currency Press.
Cover design by Emma Bennetts for Currency Press.

Currency Press acknowledges the Traditional Owners of the Country on which we live and work. We pay our respects to all Aboriginal and Torres Strait Islander Elders, past and present.

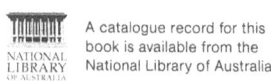
A catalogue record for this book is available from the National Library of Australia

Contents

Introduction: The clocks, the bells   *xi*
   Charlotte Wood

JULIA   1

For Lucie Charlotte, Charlie and Sam

This play is a fictional imagining by the playwright, of true events in the life of Julia Gillard. It combines references to true events, extracts from published works, interviews, fictitious commentary and opinions which the playwright and the producers believe to be honestly held. Ms Gillard has not endorsed or read, nor had any artistic input into the production of, this play.

Julia was first presented by Canberra Theatre Centre and Sydney Theatre Company, at The Playhouse, Canberra Theatre Centre, Ngunnawal Country, on 21 March 2023, and subsequently at the Drama Theatre, Sydney Opera House, Tubowgule, Gadigal Country, on 4 April 2023, with the following cast:

YOUNG WOMAN	Jessica Bentley
JULIA	Justine Clarke

Director, Sarah Goodes
Set Designer, Renée Mulder
Lighting Designer, Alexander Berlage
Composer & Sound Designer, Steve Francis
Video Designer, Susie Henderson
Assistant Director, Charley Sanders
Voice Coach, Jennifer White

Julia was commissioned by the Sydney Theatre Company.

Justine Clarke in JULIA, 2023, co-produced by Sydney Theatre Company and Canberra Theatre Centre. (Photo © Prudence Upton)

Thanks

The author would like to thank Kip Williams for first suggesting and then commissioning the writing of *Julia*, and all at Sydney Theatre Company for their support in bringing this play to the stage. Particular thanks to Sarah Goodes for her unwavering commitment to the evolution of the play and her insightful guidance, and to Justine Clarke and Jessica Bentley for their invaluable contributions during rehearsals and their faith in an untested new work. Thanks to Ruth Little, Paige Rattray and Welker White for sage advice on the script, and to the entire *Julia* company for realising so beautifully the intentions of the writing. Thanks also to Julia Gillard for allowing me to spend some invaluable time with her, despite having no assurances or control over my portrayal of her or her time in office.

Justine Clarke in JULIA, 2023, co-produced by Sydney Theatre Company and Canberra Theatre Centre. (Photo © Prudence Upton)

Introduction: The clocks, the bells

I remember the moment I learned of the fundraiser menu. I recall the room I sat in, the people I was with—women, as it happened—and I remember the sickening feeling that something precious had been wilfully smashed.

The menu, now infamous for the purity of its misogyny, was proposed for a dinner at a Brisbane restaurant. The man who wrote the words 'Julia Gillard Kentucky Fried Quail: Small Breasts, Huge Thighs & A Big Red Box' and printed them on a menu for a Liberal Party fundraiser was Joe Richards, for posterity, owner of Richards & Richards restaurant. (I name him here, for why does a woman's name forever linger after these scenarios, while the perpetrator's slides into happy anonymity?) He later apologised, calling it a private light-hearted joke between him and his son, never meant for public viewing. His apology was not to Australia's first female Prime Minister for so disgustingly insulting her, but to a Liberal MP for embarrassing him. Various male politicians feebly criticised the menu but none registered the depth of grief and rage so many women felt on reading it. Gillard's rival Kevin Rudd's response was to suggest the LNP make amends with 'a donation to the RSPCA'. Talk about adding breathtaking insult to injury.

My own response that day was visceral. My guts churned; I wept. The cherished thing that had been shattered was the last fragile shell of my hope that things were changing for women in public life in this country. But this episode showed me the grandiosity of my own delusion. You might, against all odds, rise to be elected to the country's highest position of authority—but if you have a woman's body you could expect only sleazy, deliberate, puerile contempt. This is what they had long thought of us in private; now they were gleefully saying it in public, at official events, and nobody turned a hair. The hatred not only for Prime Minister Gillard but for all women was clear, most of all in the guffawing certainty that anyone at that function reading those words would find them hilarious. *This* was what hurt: women's bodies, our intellects, our authority, our political power would never be anything but a dirty schoolboy joke. And we were fools for ever hoping otherwise.

*

I had a different physical reaction on the day of Gillard's misogyny speech. I was working at my desk at home when the texts and emails began flooding in. I watched the speech online, and the force of it propelled me out of my chair, out of my house and up the road to, of all places, the gym. I had to expel the wild energy the speech had released inside me. I listened to it in my earbuds over and over as I sweated and panted on my exercise machine. And yes, I cried again—this time with rage-filled triumph. In exhilarated solidarity with others all over the world, I felt this as a victorious moment for the women of my nation, and for Gillard herself. She had prevailed. She was *electric*.

But memory is slippery. It came as a great shock to me when, writing this introduction, I looked again at the dates. The electrifying, vanquishing speech didn't follow the hateful menu—it took place in the year *before* it. My timing was completely out. Gillard's blistering speech had changed precisely nothing—not for her, not for any of us. And when I now remember that afternoon, my unconscious choice of gym equipment is brutally ironic. I had sweated and strived, gripping the stair-stepper's handles, panting with elation at this certain turning point in my countrywomen's favour. But my steps were made into thin air, going nowhere.

*

Julia opens with clocks and warning bells, and closes with them too. This is a drama about our first woman Prime Minister—but it is also about time, and timing.

Any playwright taking on Julia Gillard's story faces some serious challenges. First, the obvious: fictionalising the private, interior life of a renowned living figure. It takes guts and world-class expertise to do this with any human decency, while also taking the liberties needed to keep the stakes high enough to make the fiction work. It's the kind of highwire act only an experienced artist can pull off and it requires both ego and humility, a combination Murray-Smith has frequently mentioned in interviews as essential for any writer.

Second, you can't write about our first female Prime Minister without bringing history—not only political history but her personal history—into play, and this requires adroit handling of *back story,* that narrative technique which, when bungled, adds a dragging weight to any drama. The tinkling harp of memory, returning us to a central character's childhood or adolescence, so often brings story creaking to a halt, losing momentum and breaking the spell of audience attention.

Third, most difficult of all, there's the fact of an already world-famous speech, written in superbly powerful language, to build into your work. How to measure up as a writer? How to give it appropriate weight and space, yet not let it eclipse the whole play?

And accompanying *that* problem, in order to allow the speech its full authority there's a whole layer of administrative dreariness to be dealt with: the workings of parliament, the arcane rules and conventions of things called standing orders and Hansard, and the intricate machinations and horse-trading leading to the defining political moment. Only a writer at the top of her game could take this stuff and not only swiftly, clearly and deftly explain it, but turn it to her advantage.

Every writer knows the application of pressure is the surest way to get the pages turning, and that the running down of the clock— hourglass as momentum—is a classic suspense technique. But in Murray-Smith's hands this is not merely technical but thematic and metaphorical. In *Julia,* time and timing underlies everything. At the opening of the play, and at its close, Julia is racing against the clock.

The deployment of time plays out in many ways. It gives us the historic momentousness of our first female leader (for me, the faint echo of Whitlam's *It's Time* can be heard beneath the surface of the text). It provides pinpoint accuracy in recent history—Peter Slipper's 'iPhone 4S' placing us in the exact year, for instance. And it gives us the heart of the play: the 1960 Six Bells Welsh coalmine disaster, its effect on Julia's father and thus on her own moral development.

I'll come back to Mr Gillard.

Another word for 'timing' is rhythm—and this playwright's switchblade command of rhythmic change is one of her secret weapons. It creates surprising tonal shifts, lending the drama its cunning humour, another vitally important dramatic device in this script. Her comic sensibility gives Murray-Smith's Julia her humanity and complexity, creating her earnest high-school debater self, her sexy eighties student activist self, her insomniac first-ginger-snap-as-prime-minister self, among others.

But there's a more devastating purpose to this humour than entertainment. It's to show us the reality gaps—the loss of innocence, the brutal undercutting and contradiction that defines Julia's career. We move with savage speed from her joyful fantasy of Australia's rapturous response to the election of its first woman PM ('The country is swathed in streamers ... posters anoint the walls of little girls across the nation, igniting new dreams, men pause in their beating of women, rap singers of the world denude the word "bitches" from their lyrics') to the repulsive reality of attacks on her womanhood, journalists' brazenly prurient speculation about her partner's sexuality, the national broadcaster's vicious, mocking sitcom. The script's ferocious humour also reveals another angle of Julia's humanity: the ambition and will to power that not only creates her, but as with all politicians in the end, destroys her.

*

Then there's her father. Oh, her father.

Julia is, of course, a play about Australia and misogyny. But like all enduring works of art, it is about many things at once. The choice of Mr Gillard as the moral centre of this play is an acutely brilliant artistic decision for many reasons, not least that in a play about the great destruction wrought by misogyny the only unblemished hero is an old white man (there's that undercutting again). The repeated line, 'All battles for justice are our battles, Julia,' haunts her as it haunts the play and leads us to what, for me, is the central theme.

'Moral injury' is the term for the deep spiritual damage to the self that takes place when we are forced, or even worse when we *choose* to betray the values we hold most dear.

The moments of greatest tension in *Julia* are those in which she must wrestle with irrevocably opposed concepts. Idealism versus pragmatism. Waiting versus acting. And the brutal fact that in politics, goodwill and integrity count for nothing unless you have the power to use them. The question for Julia is, what's the cost of that power? What does it do to a person, and is it worth it? Must she harden her heart, or was it already sufficiently steeled by ambition to turn against marriage equality, mercy for refugees, support for single parents? She repeatedly deflects doubts about her motives with a forceful, convincing defence. Without power, she persuades us, courage is 'just poetry. It's just birdsong.'

But she can't deflect forever.

The climax of the play was always going to be the speech. But for me, the deeper and broader questions come when Julia steps out of the political moment to observe just how far she has strayed from the core principles her father taught her.

'The traits you needed to qualify you for a powerful life are the same traits that disqualify you from an honourable one,' is one of the most devastating lines of the play. Soon after that, the point is wordlessly, heartbreakingly pressed home.

My father's silence.

The look in his eyes.

And there it is!

There it is, *right there.*

The price.

I know I wasn't the only honourable man's daughter weeping freely in the audience at that moment.

This framing of Mr Gillard as the play's moral guide not only illuminates the reality of a system that demands our leaders daily trample their own principles, but here provides perhaps the final provocation for that fateful day in Parliament. There's the sense that beneath the coldly political imperative, it's overwhelming fury at the insult to her father's memory that gets Julia to her feet that day, pulling the speech out of her. The unforgettable leaning into that line: 'My father *did not die of shame.*'

And so, at last, the speech. Everything till now is of course part of the swell, the slow rising of the wave. And then Murray-Smith gives it to us entire, verbatim: the whole stupendous, rolling, demolishing crescendo of it.

It's testament to the skill of the playwright that the speech feels absolutely of a piece with everything up to this moment, rather than an addition or a bubble of something new. This is achieved through precise, minute attention to language throughout the play. The mini rising crescendos, the repetitions and rhythms of political oratory have been planted for us all the way along, so that the Gillard of the real speech is at one with the fictional Julia we have seen till now. It is a brilliant accomplishment.

But most brilliant of all, Murray Smith's verbatim presentation of the speech is punctuated with pure narrative artistry—the return of the clock and the bell. All through the speech the clock winds down; the sand pours, unstoppable, through that hourglass.

One minute. Thirty seconds. Ten. It's like counting down to a rocket launch.

*

At the beginning of this introduction I said Gillard's speech in fact did nothing to save her career, changed nothing for the women of this country when she delivered it. But as I've said, one of the subjects of this play is time. And *time* changes things. It's interesting to observe, a decade on, what endures and what has fallen away. Those mediocre men and their puerile taunts have vanished into oblivion. Gillard endures as an internationally respected figure, working in arenas one hopes may be free of the spiritual self-perjury demanded by politics. Her speech endures, and now this work of art—and the questions *Julia* asks of us all—will live on, too.

Charlotte Wood, 2023

Jessica Bentley and Justine Clarke in Julia, *2023, co-produced by Sydney Theatre Company and Canberra Theatre Centre. (Photo © Prudence Upton)*

CHARACTERS

JULIA GILLARD
YOUNG WOMAN

NOTES

The speech which begins 'Let's go through the opposition leader's repulsive double standards when it comes to misogyny and sexism … ' is the verbatim speech of Julia Gillard, with some small edits.

With the exception of the recorded voices of young women at the end of the play, all voices are performed by the actor playing Julia. A second actor may be cast as the Young Woman. The use of a second actor is optional.

The present. We are nowhere or everywhere. JULIA GILLARD, *the first female Prime Minister of Australia, walks onto the dark stage. She is a little older or younger than sixty.*

JULIA GILLARD. She stands on the floor of the Chamber.

She's trembling with rage. Three words comes to her. Just three.

Three words.

It's October the ninth 2012. She's been PM for two years and four months and she's worn down. She has been hounded, slurred, dissected, libelled. She's been violated over and over again by words. She's been attacked for being too much of a woman, for not being enough of a woman. She cannot win.

And Question Time … in Parliament. It's all we've got but … it's dirty.

The Leader of the Opposition looks down at his watch.

She has very little time to make her case.

There are jeers coming from the Members behind him as she speaks.

She's shaking with purpose and for this second, she is immensely, intently, *present*.

She has a chair at the central table in front of the Speaker, beside her a chair for her deputy.

On the other side of the table is the Leader of the Opposition and beside him, a chair for his deputy.

Near them, is a small table for the Hansard reporters who record everything that is said in the Chamber, the backbone of public accountability since Thomas Curson Hansard started printing them for the British Parliament in 1802.

Surrounding the tables is horseshoe-shaped seating for up to a hundred and seventy-two Members of Parliament.

The governing party or parties sit on the right of the Chair and the Members of the Opposition on the left.

Behind the Speaker's Chair is the Coat of Arms. In front of it, sits the desk of the Clerk of the House with a button which activates the bells throughout the building.

The bells ring five minutes before the start of each sitting, before the resumption of a sitting and before any division or ballot is taken.

On the walls are clocks, two on each side of the Chamber, analogue and digital.

They indicate the time she has left. A warning light is illuminated on each clock during the final sixty seconds of her allotted time.

She remembers the words of Alfred Deakin, that a great speech cannot be prepared: 'It is the *flower* of a thought or feeling.'

A political life is so conscious. It's so 'advised'.

It's so contained. It's so *afraid*.

But in this moment, the only thing she's afraid of is running out of time.

The jeers subside and there is silence.

She seems to come to life now as she inhabits the first tense.

I'm there.

Something is driving me, some coming together—of heart and brain and history … *gathering*.

An adrenalin, a sudden freeing …

Caution's boom gate is right ahead of me but … I just *accelerate*.

'A great speech is the flower of a thought or feeling.'

And something is growing, some 'pulse inside the earth', some organic urgency, buried deep beneath the instinct to behave, pushing to the surface.

It's not just my voice.

It's a million voices inside me.

And I can feel it. I *am* it.

I look across the table at the Leader of the Opposition.

Beat.

There's the sheerest cloud of terror settling on his face. I look around and see it on the other faces in the room, colleagues and opponents ...

There's an ominous tremble in the atmosphere, the vibration of barely controlled ... rage ... in my voice.

And I'm ignited by three small words.

I will not.

   Lights change.

[*As a little girl*] 'I don't want children.'

'You will,' said my mother. 'You're only eight.'

'I will not. No. I won't.'

'That's what we do. We have children.'

'Why?'

'Well, Julia, that's a question millions of parents have asked themselves over millennia.'

'Not everyone needs to have children.'

'There wouldn't be people if people didn't make people.'

'But Mum. I want to *think*.'

'You can think *and* make people.'

'Then why do you say: "Julia be quiet: I can't hear myself think!"?'

   Lights change.

   Back to adult JULIA.

I am standing in the kitchen at Truro Avenue ...

Dad is telling me the story of Six Bells.

   Lights change.

At ten forty-five a.m. on the twenty-eighth of June 1960, three hundred metres below the surface of the earth, a spark from a falling stone ignites the coal gas at the Six Bells colliery near Abertillery in Wales.

All but three of the forty-eight men in the mine die and the town of Six Bells is devastated by the loss of its fathers and sons.

Four years after Six Bells, the Aberfan disaster sees a colliery spoil tip slide downhill and bury a hundred and sixteen children in the local school ...

The Queen comes and cries.

He looks at me, Dad. A man always and forever alive to injustice.

That quiet, mellifluous voice. The lilt.

[*Father's voice*] '*By 1913,*' he says, '*a third of all Welshmen worked in the mines, fuelling the British Empire, breathing in the soot, exposing themselves to daily catastrophe, paying for the candles that lit their way. This is how it was.*'

Dad often quoted the Welsh Labour politician Aneurin Bevan: 'The purpose of power,' he said, 'is to give it away,' and Six Bells taught me at whose feet, in this world, power deserved to be laid.

The story of Six Bells has never ... It just ... it's there.

'*All battles for justice are our battles, Julia.*'

The story which ignited my father's righteousness ignites something in me.

It's the spark.

That causes the flame. That starts the fire.

Thirty seven kilometers away from Six Bells is another Welsh town, Barry, where I was born the year after the Six Bells disaster.

[*As a teenager in debate, to herself*] Posture. Watch emotion. Enunciate. Stay on track. Focus. And KEEP CALM.

> *Directing her 'performance' to the audience she faced as a teenager.*

'As the third speaker in this debate I will use my rebuttal to summarise why "Man Should Not Lead". After all, women have always demonstrated their ability to lead, from Cleopatra to Indira Gandhi and Golda—Moir—[*Quickly correcting herself, perhaps touching her ear for memory*] My-Ear. Even if you look at sport, Evonne Goolagong is number one. On the pop charts at this very moment you will find Suzi Quatro in lead position and not far behind Sister Janet Mead with her rocking version of the Lord's Prayer.

It is a woman's diverse roles in life from the domestic to the professional that give her a far better understanding about the way the world works and how it *should* work. I would like to rebut the third speaker's suggestion that men have done a good job at leading the world for centuries. Centuries of *war*! Centuries of *violence* and *corruption*! [*Deliberate joke*] Centuries of not being able to ask directions!

Small beat and grin of self-congratulation before she goes on.

The future has a duty to be more than the past. In conclusion, women are not there to witness and applaud Man as Leader. We are there to show them how to do it! Thank you very much.'

Lights change.

I'm standing in Kathy and Lyn Pilowsky's kitchen after school and their mum, Marlene, is making tea and putting poppyseed cake on a china plate.

Her husband, Izzy, is a psychiatrist and there's something alive with possibility in their house, different to Truro Avenue.

Marlene is a fair old force of nature and she says:

'*Well, Julia, what do you have planned?*'

I don't have to think about it.

I'm going to be a teacher. Because Mr Crowe at Unley High has been ace this year. He got us writing plays.

Beat.

Mrs Pilowsky pushes the cake across the table towards me, tells Lyn to pipe down 'cause Izzy has a patient in the back room and says:

'*Your debating skills are excellent, Julia. Why not the law?*'

Graham Greene said there is one moment when the door opens and lets the future in.

Marlene Pilowsky opens that door.

At seventeen, I go back to Wales.

Our old neighbour, Mr Baker, a former coal miner, asks me what I'm going to do with my life.

'*I expect you'll get married and start a family?*' he says.

I reply that I'm going to be a lawyer and work my way up.

'*Well when you are on your way up, don't forget the flowers that grow on the roadside.*'

I tell him: I won't forget.

Change of lights.

She dances exuberantly to a soundtrack of eighties music.

The 1980s!

Everything is big. *Hair* is happening. In the US, Geraldine Ferraro becomes the first woman to be nominated as vice president by a major party. The first PCs bring the future home. For the first time our countrymen reach the top of Everest. Ambition is more than acceptable, it's admirable.

Trump's *The Art of the Deal* hits the bestseller list, along with *The G Spot*. Pat Cash and Evonne Goolagong win Wimbledon. Kylie and Danni cover Annie Lennox's 'Sisters are Doing it for Themselves' on *Young Talent Time*. Kay Cottee becomes the first woman sailor to solo circumnavigate the world non-stop, MTV rises up and the Berlin Wall comes down. Fashion is *never ever* going to be as good again.

Feminism enters the eighties a rebel—giving the finger to the mainstream establishment—and finishes the decade *firmly established as a guiding light to a better world.*

And what's hotter than a smart good-looking redhead? A smart good-looking redhead *who wants things for herself.*

I want to change the world. I really do. But I am also just … *hot*.

We're alive with the thrill of battle. We're driving around in old Chryslers, buying our clothes at disposals stores: an army of camoflaged twenty-somethings who know, deep in their strong bones, that rage is sexy. *Charged.*

Our parents aren't dead but they might as well be. The Pet Shop Boys are singing 'West End Girls' and they're in the suburbs drinking tea and making ironic murmurs about us reinventing the wheel but fuck it: this time the wheel is different!

It's *our* wheel! No tertiary fees! No multinationals! No uranium! No damming the Franklin River! And a big fucking YES to sex! The Guerrilla Girls are tackling the Art World. Naomi Wolf's *The Beauty Myth* is ready to launch. The first woman, Sandra Day O'Connor, is nominated to the Supreme Court.

Sally Ride becomes the first woman in space, defying the gravity of centuries of sexual politics.

And me. *Me too.*

I will defy gravity.

I'm acing a law degree but I'm not going to be an anonymous feminist lawyer in a city office. I'm not going to be a man, only in pantyhose and pumps.

I'm going to be … *Bigger*. I can do anything.

I can run the Australian Union of Students.

I can make deadlines, lobby, seduce, collaborate, manage a budget and excel at logistics.

I can galvanise those with barely a heartbeat.

I can fight, I can recruit, I can imagine.

I can work in corporate law and talk the talk and command the room and make money.

I can win a place in the House of Representatives.

I can give a Maiden Speech to Parliament.

I'm here for something. I'm alive to something. I'm destined for something …

Bigger.

   Beat.

[*Reminding herself*] Right?

   Beat.

[*Unsure*] I mean, I could …

   Beat.

I could—couldn't I?

[*Reminding herself*] I don't like it when … all eyes turn towards me … It's not me that matters … [*Gesturing to her body*] It's not *this* …

It's the shape of ideas. It's when the ideas hit the air. It's when they're made real by being heard. It's in the moment of *persuasion*.

What I really like is being in the messy moment, the prism of perspectives and ideologies all firing against one another and I just sneak in there with the perfect compromise.

Because I've learned a few things that I can't unlearn. Truths that are the oxygen of a political life:

Idealism without strategy is just … a figment.

I *can* jettison what I truly want for what is achievable.

I want 'the best', but I'll take 'better'.

Compromise can sometimes be heroic. *I'm a negotiator.*

And I know you're thinking: 'a negotiator'. Not exactly passionate, right?

[*With delight*] Oh. *But it is.*

That perfect place where pragmatism gets lift-off from tiny little wings of idealism …

That's the moment I'm most alive.

    Pauses, musing.

[*A revelation dawning on her, a new determination*] And for that …

[*Resolving*] … I'll stand in that light if I have to and I'll be … *luminous*.

I will shine my father's light.

It will become *my* light.

I will shine for the two of us.

    Beat.

And carried on a wave of momentum—some glorious wave of history and destiny—I prove it.

It's December third, 2007, and I am the first female Deputy Prime Minister of Australia.

Beat. She smiles.

Fuck yes.

Beat. Lights change.

My boss is now the twenty-sixth Prime Minister of Australia, an emotionally volatile Mandarin-speaking intellectual Queenslander ...

Eyebrow lift at the absurdity.

Kevin Michael Rudd.

In addition to Deputy PM I am Minister for Education, Workplace Relations and Social Inclusion. I'm the first female acting PM when Rudd travels. I get rid of the brutal Conservative initiative WorkChoices and replace it with Fair Work Australia. I'm instrumental in guiding the nation through the Global Economic Meltdown. But so far, I'm mostly famous for not buying bananas.

'Julia Gillard, then a Labor MP, is photographed in her Altona kitchen—a room utterly bereaved of personal touches. Her empty fruit bowl translates in the public consciousness as symbolic of a single career woman.'

... Murdoch.

Okay ... I see ... This is how it's going to be. Well. Fuck you and your fruit bowl. I have things to do.

And not that I have time to complain but ... the PM isn't helping.

His ego is a hand-grenade that's thrown into every room he enters. It's mayhem. I sit in my office anticipating his phone calls with dread, just like Jill Johnson in *When a Stranger Calls*, knowing there's serial killer on the loose.

The public has an inkling, but everyone in Government is under no illusions. There's an air of violence and insurrection running through Parliament because everyone knows Labor is doomed. I'm running around in a metaphorical maid's outfit cleaning up the mess.

In early May 2010, a shock jock asks me if I am going to challenge my boss, Kevin Rudd, for the leadership.

'I always expected that this year as we came into election day we would have a tough, close contest ... so I'm happy to go into that tough, close contest, side by side with Kevin Rudd ... '

'So will you promise you will not be leader at the next federal election?'

'I can, completely. Neil, this is, you know, it makes good copy for newspapers but it is not within coo-ee of my day to day reality. You may as well ask me am I anticipating a trip to Mars. No, I'm not, Neil.'

'This is all silly hypotheticals. I mean, if Steven Spielberg rang me from Hollywood and asked me to star opposite Brad Pitt in a movie, would I do it? Well, I'd be a little bit tempted. But you know what, I don't reckon Steven Spielberg *is* going to give me a call. So there's no point worrying about these sorts of hypotheticals ... '

The journos only want to know if I'll state definitively that I do not have my eyes on the prize.

[*To the radio host*] 'Sure, Jim, or Neil, or Rodney or Dennis ... whoever you are ... I'm going to tell you that I have absolutely no designs on the job. *I HAVE NO DESIGNS ON THE PRIME MINISTERSHIP.*

'We're in the game, you and me, and we both know it's a game and the listeners know it's a game. No-one is fooling anyone. *You're trying to get a tasty soundbite to fill airspace between the ads for carpet. You're baiting me to say what you want but ...*

'*I will not.*

'*I'm* denying everything because like all politicians, I'm dedicated to telling the truth only when it serves me.

'Come on, Neil! You *know* I'm seeking the office! You *know* I'll say whatever is required to win the game! And you *know* I'll say to you that I'm behind Kevin oh-seven twenty-four-seven.

'It's *your* job to suggest. And it's *my* job to deny.'

[*To the audience*] It seems as if everyone hates the PM.

Everyone.

And politicians don't 'bay' for blood. *They're quietly ravenous.*

We all know what I cannot say. That if anyone should have the job it's me. Because I've been holding the shit-show together with extraordinary aplomb.

And quite frankly, it's embarrassing that there have been sixty-one global female leaders since 1960 but there's never been a woman in the job in this country.

[*Addressing the radio host again, with triumph in her voice*] 'So when I say that asking me if I'd challenge is like asking me if I'm going to Mars, we both know that the rockets are firing, buckle up, Kevin's on death row *and I AM FUCKING GOING TO MARS.*'

    Beat.

[*With a little disappointment*] Obviously, I don't say that.

But when on the twenty-fourth of June 2010, the parliamentary party votes on whether or not to retain Kevin Rudd as leader, the party knows the Labor government will not last with Kevin.

He is, after all: '*A once in a century egomaniac.*'

Those are the words of the previous Labor leader, Mark Latham, in the *Guardian* … Total nut-job himself!

Like Latham, Kevin has never met a spotlight he didn't gravitate to. An insatiable scene-stealer, he has a truly astonishing talent to cosy up to the media … His endless Twitter-fest, his self-promoting public statements … Popping into the newsrooms of the major newspapers, tweeting greetings from his hospital bed *whilst having surgery*—who the fuck does that?

His entire existence is a metaphorical selfie.

The media reports of his mid-air tantrums don't help. He ordered a vegetarian meal which was not forthcoming.

Poor hostie was in floods. But I mustn't go on.

    Beat. Chuckles with pleasure.

Well. All right!

The time he went bonkers at the Copenhagen Climate Summit:

'*Those Chinese fuckers are trying to rat-fuck us.*'

That man is poetry in motion!

>   *Beat.*

I throw the dice. Wednesday evening I tell him I'm going to challenge. He plans to fight by contesting a leadership poll.

I thrill to politics. But I also thrill to poker. Both require two things: a carefully curated face to the world—and mathematics. A straight flush comes only once in sixty-five thousand hands, but when it goes to the Party Room I know I won't need a straight flush. I just need three of a kind to his two pair.

And it's looking good. *But for one thing.*

People don't like a coup behind closed doors, especially if, when the door opens, there's a woman standing there.

A good woman, a *womanly* woman will defer. She'll recognise her duty to freeze permanently in second position.

Her obligation is to never initiate change when the status quo is male. A man is focussed and determined. A woman is devious. The very definition of femininity is to uphold male authority even if it has no hope of leading the party to victory. *Because a woman is best at making a man feel better.*

My attitude is … No.

Just … No.

By Thursday morning, Kevin, reading the writing on the wall, loses 'heart' and withdraws from the challenge.

>   *Beat.*

And just like that. I am PM.

>   *Long beat.*

[*Pensive, thoughtful*] I should be happy.

>   *Beat … Doubt … wondering why she isn't.*

That night, I lie in bed, unable to sleep. For years, I've been going to sleep wondering how to get what I want … We all do, we politicians … We drift off to … strategy.

But my head's on the pillow and ... *I have what I want.*

The only thing that can happen now is ... that I lose it.

And it's not *if* but *when*.

That's my first thought: From the second you sit on the throne, they're plotting to get rid of you.

That's just ... how it is.

I make a cup of tea. I think to myself something stupid. Along the lines of: 'The is the first cup of tea I'm making as Prime Minister.'

'It's my first two a.m. as Prime Minister.'

'It's my first Butternut Snap as Prime Minister' ...

You get the picture.

I think about all the moments that led me here, the incidental influences and accidental turns that stealthily built my path. Mum and Dad. Me and the Pilofsky sisters at Glenelg beach. Me and Alison watching *The Twilight Zone* at midnight. Things spoken and heard in the kitchen at Truro Avenue ...

The story of Six Bells ... The story of the town, the widows, the orphans ...

My father's words, alive with grief ...

The Welsh poet, Gillian Clarke, wrote a poem to commemorate the fiftieth anniversary of the disaster.

'Perhaps a woman hanging out the wash
paused, hearing something, a sudden hush,

a pulse inside the earth like a blow to the heart,
holding in her arms the wet weight

of her wedding sheets, his shirts. Perhaps
heads lifted from the work of scrubbing steps,

hands stilled from wringing rainbows onto slate,
while below the town, deep in the pit

a rock-fall struck a spark from steel, and fired
the void, punched through the mine a fist

of blazing firedamp. As they died,
perhaps a silence, before sirens cried,

before the people gathered in the street,
before she'd finished hanging out her sheets.'

I close my eyes …

She's in the backyard, lifting the washing, poised for calamity. Pulling off her apron, she starts running, joining the hectic footfalls of the doomed women down Somerset Street. The wives and the sisters clinging to the steel gates, waiting, in silence.

Beat.

I'm lying there in bed as dawn breaks, with my second Butternut Snap as PM.

I can hear a distant siren, frightening the night. And a dog barking. It's cold. My throat hurts from talking … I've been talking for weeks, persuading, denying, explaining, selling …

Beat.

I am alone.

Beat.

Despite Tim.

Despite the party colleagues. Despite Jacqui and Kathy and Lyn. Despite Mum and Dad.

She is alone. The woman at the washing line. The news travelling towards her. Her life changing in a second.

As is mine. Now.

And what is travelling toward me?

Lights change. Long beat.

[*With new energy*] '*Yet who would have thought the old man to have so much blood in him?*'

Kevin's out. I'm in.

If any male politician wins a leadership spill, it's all part of the cut-and-thrust of politics. When it's a woman: she's Lady Macbeth.

'*Many suggest she has blood on her hands.*' … Murdoch.

[*Playing up to it*] They see me … eyes ablaze, a psychopathic stare, my hands clasping his neck, blocking the carotid arteries and the jugular so his deoxygenated blood can't exit the brain. His eyes are bulging with the awareness that he is taking his final breath, a cloud of red shimmering in front of him … limbs jerking as my neatly manicured fingers press on his blood vessels, until he drops, lifeless, to the floor.

Deed done.

Beat.

I calmly lift one polished navy pump off the carpet tile and crush his spectacles under foot, splintering the glass, because—

A wry giggle.

he won't be needing them again.

The King is dead. Long live the … Queen.

Beat.

In truth? No psychopathic stare. No Shakespearean overtures or asphyxiation. Just another moment in politics where one single element proves paramount: *timing*.

It's timing that invites pragmatism, opportunism and destiny into the room. Come on in. Make yourselves at home!

The roof of Parliament House encloses every variation of the human instinct to exploit the moment.

Traitorous acts, grinning duplicity, the tidy compartmentalisation of morals. They will happen when the moment presents itself.

And yes, in politics … we will kill if the timing is right.

But we're no Macbeth! Macbeth felt regret!

I won't regret anything that clears the way. Not now. Not yet.

I will not.

Our only regrets are for the moments we display frailty, naivete, tenderness … Love, even. The distracted moments when we forget the mission, the *only* mission, the mission above all else, the mission to *survive*.

Because in politics, we never regret anything that … works.

I didn't need to kill Kevin. Kevin's death was suicide by ego.

But—so you know—
If we must dip our oars in blood as we sail into the future,
Swish through its viscous crimson tide,
To get where we must go,
We will do so.
We will steer that vessel,
Blood dripping from its hull,
Beach it,
And delete the voyage from memory.

Beat. Lights change.

The twenty-seventh and first female Prime Minister of Australia. Sworn in by the first female Governor-General. Two chicks.

But the clock is ticking. It's always ticking … Later, Paul Keating, ex-PM, will say to me '*We all get carried out in a box, love.*' I can't see the box yet.

But I know it will come for me. And I have to get things done first.

Beat.

'*Yet who would have the thought the old man to have so much blood in him?*'

No-one was going to let me forget I stepped over the corpse of a man to get power.

But really … Does a woman have any other choice?

I was in a position no man would be required to defend but I was under no illusions. It was no good getting the vote of my party. I needed the legitimacy of 'the people's vote'.

I had to drown out the call of 'Traitor'.

I had to drown out the call of 'Pretender'.

And it wasn't just the voters I had to convince. *I* needed to know I earned my place through the ballot box, not the backroom dealing.

I had to call an election and win.

'*I ... acknowledge I have not been elected Prime Minister by the Australian people. And in coming months I will ask the Governor-General to call for a general election so that the Australian people can exercise their birthright to choose their Prime Minister.*'

Lights change.

Of the House of Representatives' one hundred and fifty seats, the coalition wins seventy-three.

We win seventy-two.

No-one has a majority.

I am standing on the edge of a cliff and the conservatives are whipping up gale-force winds.

As I balance on that precipice, below me the yawning void of legacy, I absorb every tiny shift in wind direction and I understand with terrifying clarity that *my power is entirely at the mercy of others.*

I need the backing of the Greens and three independents. I'm persuasive. I'm dogged. And I get their backing.

I win. Just.

The first hung parliament since 1940.

But we have one more card up our sleeve to secure it. Peter Slipper, Speaker of the House, who maintains the order and protocols during debates, who is traditionally a person of considerable parliamentary status—he will back me to shore up our majority.

Only by October ninth 2012, Peter Slipper has just fucked himself royally.

When he rolls up in official dress, he has a modicum of dignity. But in civvies, often a grey suit with a wide striped green tie and service-station sunnies, he looks more like someone who imports heroin in coconuts.

A married man in his sixties, Slipper texts his media adviser, James Ashby, a man in his thirties.

It must have been a slow day for Slipper because he texts his advisor about vaginas:

'They look like a mussel removed from its shell. Look at a bottle of mussel meat. Salty Cunts in brine.'

On hearing the ping of his new iPhone 4s, Ashby is about to become a grimy smudge of a footnote in the annals of history.

The texts are leaked. Obviously.

Australians are not, by nature puritanical. But no-one likes the C-word. It's just a bit … nasty. And nobody wants a Speaker of the House who free associates seafood with genitalia.

The outcry is immediate. The 'Slipper Affair' becomes the biggest news story of my Prime Ministership. And leading the charge is Tony Abbott, Leader of the Opposition, his face invariably etched in an affable grin. A blokey grin. A 'Come on now, have a sense of humour, love' grin.

Tony Abbott.

A curious little guy.

A monarchist, obviously.

In favour of ditching no-fault divorce.

Notably remarked that climate change is '*probably doing good; or at least, more good than harm.*'

Anti-stem cell research and euthanasia 'cause euthanasia's there to reduce suffering and he's more or less dedicated his life to increasing it.

Described a government bill to decriminalise abortion as '*infanticide on demand*' making murderers of young women …

Despite all this … he's not actually a terrible person. His convictions may be nuts, but at least he has convictions.

The party doesn't love Tony.

   Beat.

But he's all they've got.

Slipper has to go. But I don't do lynch mobs and my feeling is: Let the man pop on his gowns one last time to say he's sorry, brought shame, beg forgiveness from his long suffering missus and resign in order to take up some position *where misogyny and hypocrisy are vital qualifications.*

But Peter Slipper had resigned from the Liberal Party to become Speaker and therefore had supplied us with one vital extra ally. So Tony Abbott wants him gone. Not because of his misogynistic text messages. But because Slipper helped us secure our very fragile majority.

Slipper had betrayed them and they want revenge.

With no choice, Slipper enters the house, takes the chair and resigns. And asks his long-suffering wife for forgiveness and … goes on to become *a priest.*

Beat. Lights change.

The first female prime minister of the nation.

I make a promise to myself, a promise I now regret: that I am never going to talk 'sexism'.

I don't want to preface every statement with 'as a woman'.

I don't care about 'as a woman'.

I don't want to live inside inverted commas …

And men hate women talking about sexism. Not because they're threatened. Because it bores them.

She looks at a man in the audience.

Admit it. You were riveted before but now you're bored …

She turns back to the general audience.

Was there ever a less interesting word than 'sexism'?

It's boring to have to think about it. It's boring to have to live with it. It's boring to talk about it. Women generally hate talking about sexism.

So why do we do it? Because *why should men get to be fuckwits and then live in peace?* If we can't *change* you, at least we can *bore you to death.*

But it's different for me. Because any time a powerful woman draws attention to what it takes to succeed she is accused of playing 'the Gender Card'.

I can see the headlines:

'*PM deflects criticism by claiming victimhood!*'

I'm not going to hand them that on a plate!

Raising sexism *never* deflects criticism, it only increases it.

So keep quiet.

    Beat. Lights change.

The joy that meets my success! Elected by the people!

The country is swathed in streamers! Placards are held in town squares by almost all of the twelve million women in the country stating: 'FINALLY!'—a bi-partisan force of feminist euphoria.

Dead White Males tweet: '*You Go Girl!*' The belittling taunts of little boys in playgrounds are suddenly hushed, posters of my face anoint the walls of little girls across the nation, igniting new dreams, men pause in their beating of women, rap singers the world over denude the word 'bitches' from their lyrics and in the department stores of a nation, no man purchases a single birthday Dyson.

The rightwing media pause the flow of vitriol for a moving moment of philosophical reflection: '*Let's just be nicer!*'

The tabloids' front pages shout:

'*It's a Girl!*'

The boards of men's clubs have simultaneous epiphanies, editorials rhapsodise over my resilience, for fighting the battles, for smiling through the sexist slurs, for being patronised, laughed at, denigrated and demeaned.

Alan Jones thanks me for teaching men the humility that leads to wisdom and oh my God, the flowers Rupert and Wendi with an 'i' send me! Seriously … lilies, roses and a card that reads: '*Welcome to Power. It's fun here!*'

    Lights change. Beat.

[*Voice of radio interviewer*] '*Julia, is Tim moving into the Lodge?*'

[*Her own voice, disbelieving*] '*What?*'

[*Voice of radio interviewer*] '*Tim? Your partner? Is he bunking down with you in the PM's lodging?*'

[*Her own voice*] Why wouldn't he? Also ... Why is everyone calling me 'Julia'? Did you call Prime Minister Howard 'John'? Did you call Prime Minister Rudd, 'Kev'? I'm not asking for anything special ...

Howard Sattler. Broadcaster on 6PR: '*Tim's gay.*'

'Well that's absurd.'

[*Voice of radio interviewer*] '*But you hear it. He must be gay he's a hairdresser. It's not me saying it.*'

[*Her own voice*] 'That's ridiculous—'

[*Voice of radio interviewer*] '*You can confirm that he's not?*'

[*Her own voice*] 'Howard, don't be ridiculous.'

[*Voice of radio interviewer*] '*But is it a heterosexual relationship? That's all I'm asking.*'

[*To audience*] Imagine him asking John Howard about Janette?

'*PM, Can you confirm Janette bats for the ladies?*'

[*Howard's voice*] '*Janette and I enjoy the missionary position, Howard, which is more than adequate for me to climax. And if I climax, Janette's happy.*

That's just how we roll.'

[*Her own voice*] Channel Nine news quotes an image consultant on my jacket: '*She was three days into office, it honestly looked like a cheap motel bedspread.*'

I'm ridiculed after the *Women's Weekly* publishes a photo of me knitting a toy kangaroo for the royal baby '*with her pet caboodle Reuben at her feet. References to Nero fiddling while Rome burns abound.*'

' ... *Gillard revels in her otherness: living the austere lifestyle of a woman with none of the usual aspirations such as settling down, getting married, having children. Her kitchen is bare. She struggles with tongs at a barbecue. On the ABC's* Australian Story *last week she said she can manage only one focus: politics.*'

Germaine Greer, ground-breaking feminist and one of the world's leading intellectuals, opines on national TV:

[*Greer's voice*] '*What I want her to do is get rid of those bloody jackets. Every time she turns around you've got that strange horizontal crease, which means they're cut too narrow in the hips ...* '

'*You've got a big arse, Julia, now get on with it! ...* '

[*Her own voice*] When they can't destroy me any other way, the conservative press argues I'm a self-indulgent first-world whiner who doesn't know what real sexism is.

They argue real sexism belongs to Afghanistan, Pakistan, Iran because, God knows, they've hitherto shown such compassion for those countries.

Columnist Janet Albrechtsen ... Murdoch:

    Beat.

'*Today's feminists feast at a smorgasbord of whinges, whines, victimhood claims, misogyny games, gender binary discussions, western world obsessions about pay gaps and quotas and glass ceilings.*'

And when *her* daughter is harassed at work, paid less than her male colleagues, felt up, intimidated, threatened, insulted? Does she say: *Stop complaining, you're not in Kabul?*

What is ... ?

Where does this ... ?

No-one blinks when the national broadcaster airs the first satirical sitcom about a sitting prime minister. An actress in a red wig and ugly jacket.

Be silent, Julia.

Alan Jones on the highest rating breakfast radio show in the country:

'*And quite frankly, they should shove her and Bob Brown into a chaff bag and take them as far out to sea as they can and tell them to swim home.*'

One Conservative announced that I '*was unfit for leadership*' because I was '*deliberately barren*'.

Unfit for leadership because I was deliberately barren.

This tiny private essence of myself, shielded from view ... so private and mysterious that even I can not quite explain it to myself, just something I know, have always known ... used like a ...

Scalpel.

Julia. Just ... keep quiet. The main course on a menu at a Liberal National Party fundraiser stated: '*Julia Kentucky Fried Quail—small breasts, huge thighs and a big red box*' ...

Beat.

In the most inhospitable political climate imaginable, with barely a majority, I get five hundred and seventy bills passed by the Senate. *The highest record of legislation passed in the history of Federal Parliament.* Higher than Hawke. Much higher than Howard. Or Menzies. The National Disability Insurance Scheme. The implementation of the carbon price. Education reforms. Paid parental leave. The implementation of the National Broadband Network. The child abuse royal commission.

I got things done. I did it fast. And I did it with the barest grasp on power.

That takes passion. That takes resilience.

Five hundred and seventy bills. And still they called me 'Julia'.

Beat.

Was this the price?

Realising that the country I loved was built on a pervasive contempt for women: mothers, servants, quick fucks, deliverers of the overcooked tea, the Colonial woman in the bush shack imprisoned by the eucalypts, the nuns in schools whipping small masturbators, the grinning mum with washing powder and soiled sport shorts ... A nation built on whores or angels ... Keeping the stage empty for—*men.*

Beat. She thinks ...

I've got what I wished for. And I don't think that—even for a second—I don't doubt for a second that I should be here.

But enduring this …

Is this the price? Or—or—

Something even worse …

Finding that the traits you needed to qualify you for a powerful life, are the same traits that disqualify you from an honorable one?

Beat as the thought grows, takes hold.

What has … become of me?

Am I still—? Am I—?

Mum says: '*We know who you are. You know who you are.*'

But do I?

Beat.

The ordinary men and woman who see raising good kids as the real achievement.

No big dreams, no illusions, no promises …

Mum. Dad.

Marlene and Izzy Pilowsky. Mr Crowe from Unley High.

Mr Baker, who told me to notice the flowers when I was seventeen.

Eighty, ninety years of … setting a very tiny compass true north …

Can I be that any more?

Because I'm living a life that's a fight to the death.

Inside this Chamber … friends, enemies alike, we have sacrificed modesty. We have thrown our hat in the game, regardless of cost. And our will to love has contracted to make space for our need to survive.

The school concerts missed. The Mother's Days and eightieths, the Sunday lunches, the first steps, the whooping cough scare in the middle of the night, the reunion, last words at bedsides, the old friend's wedding, the ordinary nights of nothing special.

A catalogue of things unwitnessed, unfelt, ungiven.

In this extraordinary life, the ordinary becomes … surreal.

And this makes you just a tiny bit less … *human.*

Is that the price?

I'm asking the question.

And it's a question I'm never going to ask again.

　Long beat.

[*Troubled*] Asylum seekers are arriving in leaky boats via people smugglers.

Iraq, Congo, Myanmar, Syria, Afghanistan, Ethiopia, Eritrea, Iran, Bhutan ...

Terrified, tortured, fractured, stateless.

The kitchen in Truro Avenue. I remember his voice.

'*All battles for justice are our battles, Julia.*'

　Long beat.

[*Determined*] I'm resuming offshore processing.

I'm reopening offshore detention centres.

Those who don't fit in the detention centres on Nauru and Manus Island, can live here on a 'bridging visa' but they can't work.

Potential terrorists Drowning children Open the floodgates People smugglers Queue jumpers Children terrorists Floodgate potential Potential jumpers Drowning terrorists Potential children Drowning queues Terrorist floodgates Jumping children ...

[*Defensive*] I'm not heartless, but ... there are complexities.

I have to commit to 'fair, orderly migration'.

The underpinning of a hardline approach *is* fundamentally humane. We don't want them drowning.

[*To the audience*] '*All battles for justice are our battles, Julia.*'

He knows I have a job to do and he knows it's difficult.

He knows I care, Dad. He knows I do care. He knows I'm a compassionate person.

Of course I am, he made me.

And he's going to back me no matter what.

Because what good is courage if it costs you power? Courage *needs* power or it's irrelevant. It's just poetry. It's just birdsong. It's just a love note.

Power turns courage into change. Without power, it's just a figment.

Politics is a persuasion and sometimes with persuasion you do what you have to do. You say what you need to say. So you get what you need.

Besides … regret just takes up space for … action.

Beat.

So no to the refugees.

No to marriage equality.

Yes to a reduction in the single parent benefit …

Beat.

My father's silence.

The look in his eyes.

And there it is!

There it is, *right there.*

The price.

Beat.

And then—

Long beat. New moment.

He dies.

Beat.

I read Dylan Thomas.

Those lines my father read aloud of *Dead Men Naked*:

' … *Though they sink through the sea they shall rise again …*
Though lovers be lost love shall not;
And death shall have no dominion … '

Death has dominion over me.

I have been robbed.

[*Confessional*] Death is silence. It's absence.
It's a wrestle with time.
It's a Rolodex of fragments. It's cold nights just me and him.
It's petulance at nature.
It's his fugitive face in dreams.
It's fury-making tea at three a.m.
It's wonder at the split second shift from breath to none,
From the chirpy persistence of the hospital ward to
The silence of the mortuary fridge.
I hold his warm hand and then—
He is underground.

Beat.

Nothing else is irrevocable.

Beat.

But death …
Just. Won't. Listen.

Beat.

[*New energy*] Knowing I am safely tucked away at home mourning my father, Kevin pops onto *The 7.30 Report*. Just because.

And while Kevin is basking in the glow of the studio lights, shock jock Alan Jones entertains the great and good of the Liberal Party at a fundraiser:

Beat.

'The old man died a few weeks ago of shame. To think that he had a daughter who told lies every time she stood for Parliament.'

I can fight. I'm very fucking resilient.

Beat. Wipes away a tear.

At seven, you think: 'If only I can make it through this shit-show of childhood, I'll come out the other side where people have learned how to behave.' And then you get there. To adulthood … And *no-one* knows the fuck how to behave.

'Must have died of shame' …

Maybe that's why teenagers are so difficult. Because they approach adulthood realising that it's the same kind of shit-show as childhood, only now the bullies hold the world in the palms of their hands.

What do you do with that?

You believe that morality turns the handle that spins the world. That people are fundamentally good. That the world honours the heroes and the villains get found out.

What do you do?

When it turns out to be a lie and you're part of the system that makes it a lie?

Beat.

But I'll tell you what.

John Gillard did not die of shame.

Long beat as she contemplates her ledger of wins and losses:

I know what I believe.

I know what I've done. I know what I failed to do.

I know how certain I sound when all I'm feeling is doubt.

I know what I've lost—so much I just haven't noticed.

I know the loss of tender time-wasting, of exploring, of being a mystery to myself.

There has been no time to linger there.

I know the love I haven't felt.

I know the absence of nature … Those flowers by the roadside … All of them …

Missed.

Beat.

But I found things too.

I believe the world is flawed but that it is beautiful.

I believe it is more the outcome of great instincts than terrible ones.

I believe that we can work to make it better because human beings are graceful and creative.

I believe that.

I believe there is purpose in telling our stories.

I believe in voices rising up. I will not be silent.

I will not.

Lights change.

It's October ninth, 2012.

Later this day, Peter Slipper will resign. But in the end, ironically, the day is not about him.

I've been PM for two years and four months and I'm worn down. I have been hounded, slurred, dissected, libeled. I've been destroyed for being a woman, for not being enough of a woman.

The creepy red hair. The wide arse.

The empty fruit bowl. The shitty tailoring. Barren.

Ditch the witch! Burn her ...

Venom has sprinted through the veins of commercial radio, Murdoch minions, right-wing Barbie dolls, professional tweeters, giggling at their talent for crucifixion, high on the speed of the send button.

And then there's Question Time ...

Every parliamentary week, I have to prepare myself for the onslaught of ridicule, abuse, paranoia, strategic subterfuge and pure politics of Question Time.

I have a folder, put together by my advisers, with all likely topics, questions and hand grenades the opposition might lob at me. You find out stuff about people in Question Time. How far they'll go.

The advisers advise:

'*It's going to be Slipper. They're going to want to take him down and you down with him—*'

In 1992, PM Paul Keating, a man who uses language like a switchblade, redefined the tone of Question Time with his riposte to the opposition leader John Hewson's question about why he hadn't called an early election '*Because I wanna do you slowly.*'

I'm in the colosseum and *everyone* I'm addressing is a lion. They've been hungry for blood all week and now I stand to take the floor. And I know they're gonna do me slowly, so that I experience maximum pain before losing consciousness.

It's *Halloween* meets *Texas Chainsaw Massacre*, only in suits.

As usual this afternoon, I take my seat opposite Mr Abbott, who rises to move a motion.

[*Speaking as Tony Abbott*] *'I say to this Prime Minister, just as the Speaker has failed the character test, you, Prime Minister, have failed the judgement test. I must allude to the vile anatomical references to which this Speaker appears to be addicted in his text messaging ... Let us be absolutely crystal clear about the situation in this parliament right now.*

This Speaker is this Prime Minister's creation. This Speaker's actions are the Prime Minister's responsibility and this Speaker's standards perforce are this Prime Minister's standards ... '

[*Her own voice*] What the flying fuck?

He's going to take the moral high ground? *Him? He's* going to cast doubt on my standards? Him? Who stood in front of men holding signs calling me those vile things. A WITCH. A BITCH. He stood in front of those signs on national television, *giving the nation permission.*

Did he say: '*This kind of disgusting and demeaning rhetoric has no place in a decent society*'?

Did he say: '*This language would never be used against a male politician and it should not be used against the female Prime Minister of Australia or indeed any woman*'?

Did he say: '*I am embarrassed by these signs. I am embarrassed for what they say about this country's attitudes to women*'?

Tony Abbott said nothing.

    Beat.

Three daughters.

    Beat.

Abbott is staring at me, the slight tilt of his mocking grin ...

For someone so arrogant, he has a diffidence that makes me feel sorry for him.

A man like that is always going shoulder to shoulder with the winds of change.

But I am change.

There I am. The Speaker ... the clocks ... the Hansard recorders ... The advisors in the distance, faces mouthing the words ... The press ... the Opposition hungry for my ... tears ...

'Small breasts, huge thighs and a big red box' ...

>*Beat.*

No.

>*Beat.*

Fuck silence.

You can tell me to be silent but ...

I Will Not.

>*Beat.*

'*We're all carried out in a box, love.*'

Yes, we are.

But for the blink of an eyelash in the history of time, we're here for something.

And right now ... there's a rumbling ... Something '*paused ... a sudden hush, a pulse inside the earth like a blow to the heart*'.

Something ... pure of purpose, an adrenalin, a sudden freeing ... And it's rising through me ... It's rising ... Some deep rhythmic thrill. A blow to the heart ...

That starts it.

>*Lights change. The hubbub of the political chamber: white noise voices fading as she speaks ...*
>
>*Her attention and tone go from the general to the specific moment and location. She looks around the audience as if they are sitting in the Chamber of Parliament House.*

Thank you very much Deputy Speaker and I rise to oppose the motion moved by the Leader of the Opposition, and in so doing I say to the Leader of the Opposition: I will not be lectured about sexism and misogyny by this man. I will not. And the government will not be lectured about sexism and misogyny by this man, not now, not ever. The Leader of the Opposition says that people who hold sexist views and who are misogynists are not appropriate for high office. Well, I hope the Leader of the Opposition has a piece of paper and he is writing out his resignation, because if he wants to know what misogyny looks like in modern Australia he does not need a motion in the House of Representatives; he needs a mirror … That's what he needs …

Let's go through the opposition leader's repulsive double standards—repulsive double standards—when it comes to misogyny and sexism. We are now supposed to take seriously that the Leader of the Opposition is offended by Mr Slipper's text messages, when this is what the Leader of the Opposition said—and this was when he was a minister under the last government, not when he was a student, not when he was in high school but when he was a minister under the last government.

He has said, and I quote: 'In a discussion about women being underrepresented in institutions of power in Australia, the interviewer was a man called Stavros and the Leader of the Opposition said: "If it's true, Stavros, that men have more power, generally speaking, than women, is that a bad thing?"'

And then a discussion ensues and another person being interviewed says, 'I want my daughter to have as much opportunity as my son,' to which the Leader of the Opposition says 'Yeah, I completely agree, but what if men are by physiology or temperament more adapted to exercise authority or to issue command?' Then ensues another discussion about women's role in modern society, and the other person participating in the discussions says, 'I think it's very hard to deny that there is an underrepresentation of women,' to which the Leader of the Opposition says, 'But now there's an assumption that this is a bad thing.' This is the man from whom we are supposed to take lectures about sexism!

And then of course it goes on. I was very offended personally when the Leader of the Opposition as minister for health said—and I quote: 'Abortion is the easy way out.' I was very personally offended by those comments. You said that in March 2004, and I suggest you check the records.

I was also very offended on behalf of the women of Australia when in the course of the carbon pricing campaign the Leader of the Opposition said, 'What the housewives of Australia need to understand as they do the ironing.' Thank you for that painting of women's role in modern Australia ... Then, of course, I was offended too by the sexism, by the misogyny, of the Leader of the Opposition catcalling across this table at me as I sit here as Prime Minister, 'if the Prime Minister wants to, politically speaking, make an honest woman of herself' something that would never have been said to any man sitting in this chair.

I was offended when the Leader of the Opposition went outside in the front of the Parliament and stood next to a sign that said 'Ditch the witch'. I was offended when the Leader of the Opposition stood next to a sign that described me as a man's bitch. I was offended by those things.

It is misogyny, sexism, every day from this Leader of the Opposition. Every day, in every way, across the time the Leader of the Opposition has sat in that chair and I have sat in this chair, that is all we have heard from him.

Now the Leader of the Opposition wants to be taken seriously.

Apparently he has woken up, after this track record and all of these statements, he's woken up and has gone, 'Oh dear, there is this thing called sexism; oh my lord, there is this thing called misogyny. Now, who is one of them? The Speaker must be because that suits my political purpose.' Doesn't turn a hair about any of his past statements; doesn't walk into this parliament and apologise to the women of Australia; does not walk into this parliament and apologise to me for the things that have come out of his mouth, but he now seeks to use this as a battering ram against someone else. Well, this kind of hypocrisy should not be tolerated ... Which is why this motion from the Leader of the Opposition should not be taken seriously.

And then second, the Leader of the Opposition is always wonderful at walking into this parliament and giving me and others a lecture about what they should take responsibility for. He is always keen to say others should assume responsibility, particularly me.

Well, can anybody remind me whether the Leader of the Opposition has taken any responsibility for the conduct of the Sydney Young Liberals and the attendance at their event of members of his front bench? Has he taken any responsibility for the conduct of members of his political party and members of his front bench, who apparently when the most vile things were being said about my family raised no voice of objection. No-one walked out of the room, no-one walked up to Mr Jones and said that this was not acceptable.

Instead, it was all viewed as good fun until it was run in a Sunday newspaper, and then the Leader of the Opposition and others started ducking for cover. Big on lectures on responsibility; very light on accepting responsibility himself for the vile conduct of members of his political party.

Third, Ms Deputy Speaker, why the Leader of the Opposition should not be taken seriously on this motion. The Leader of the Opposition and the Deputy Leader of the Opposition have come into this place and have talked about the member for Fisher.

Well, let me remind the opposition, and the Leader of the Opposition particularly ... about their track record and association with the Member of Fisher.

I remind them that ... the Liberal Party preselected Mr Slipper for the 1993 election.

Then for the '96 election. Then for the '98 election. Then for the 2001 election. Then for the 2004 election.

Then for the 2007 election and then for the 2010 election.

And across many of those preselections Mr Slipper enjoyed the personal support of the Leader of the Opposition ... I remind the Leader of the Opposition, who now comes in here and speaks about

Mr Slipper and apparently his inability to work with or talk to Mr Slipper. I remind the Leader of the Opposition he attended Mr Slipper's wedding.

Did he walk up to Mr Slipper in the middle of the service and say he was disgusted to be there? Was that the attitude he took? No, He attended that wedding as a friend. The Leader of the Opposition keen to lecture others about what they ought to know or did know about Mr Slipper. Well, with respect, I would say to the Leader of the Opposition that, after a long personal association, including attending Mr Slipper's wedding, it would be interesting to know whether the Leader of the Opposition was surprised by these text messages.

He is certainly in a position to speak more intimately about Mr Slipper than I am. Then, of course, the Leader of the Opposition comes into this place and says:

And I quote: every day the Prime Minister stands in this Parliament to defend this Speaker will be another day of shame for this Parliament; another day of shame for a government which should already have died of shame.

Well, can I indicate to the Leader of the Opposition that the government is not dying of shame—and my father did not die of shame. What the Leader of the Opposition should be ashamed of is his performance in this Parliament and the sexism he brings with it. Now ... On the conduct of Mr Slipper and on the text messages which are in the public domain. I have seen the press reports of those text messages and I am offended by their content. I am offended by their content because I am always offended by sexism. I am offended by their content because I am always offended by statements which are anti women. I am offended by those things in the same way I have been offended by things the Leader of the Opposition has said and no doubt will continue to say in the future because if this, today, was an exhibition of his new feminine side, I do not think we have much to look forward to in terms of changed conduct. And I am offended by those text messages. But what I will not stand for, what I will never stand for is the Leader of the Opposition coming into this place and peddling a double standard.

Peddling a standard for Mr Slipper he would not set for himself ... I will not ever allow the Leader of the Opposition to impose his double standards on this Parliament.

A YOUNG WOMAN *appears on stage.*

YOUNG WOMAN: One minute, thirty.

JULIA *continues her speech.*

JULIA: Sexism should always be unacceptable.

We should conduct ourselves as it should always be, unacceptable. The Leader of the Opposition says, 'Do something.' Well, he could do something himself if he wanted to deal with sexism in this Parliament. He could change his behaviour, he could apologise for his past statements and he could apologise for standing next to signs describing me as a witch and a bitch—terminology now objected to by the front-bench of the opposition. He could change standards himself if he sought to do so.

But we will see none of that from the Leader of the Opposition, because on these questions he is incapable of change. He is capable of double standards but incapable of change. His double standards should not rule this Parliament.

Good sense, common sense and proper process are what should rule this Parliament. That is what I believe is the path forward for this Parliament, not the kinds of double standards and political game playing imposed by the Leader of the Opposition, who is now looking at his watch because, apparently, a woman has spoken for too long. I have had him yell at me to shut up in the past!

YOUNG WOMAN: Thirty seconds ...

JULIA: But I will take the remaining, I will take the remaining seconds of my speaking time to say to the Leader of the Opposition that I think the best course for him is to reflect on the standards he has exhibited in public life, on the responsibility he should take for his public statements, on his close personal connection with Peter Slipper and on the hypocrisy he has displayed in this House today.

YOUNG WOMAN: Ten ...

JULIA: And on that basis, because of the Leader of the Opposition's motivations, this Parliament should today reject this motion, and the Leader of the Opposition should think seriously about the role of women in public life and in Australian society because we are entitled to a better standard than this.

> *She takes a moment to walk away and sit down, or to turn away, indicating the end of that reality.*
>
> *We are now outside that moment.*

YOUNG WOMAN:
The woman working in the blast furnace in Port Kembla.
The lawyer in Cottesloe.
The girl on the bicycle in Fitzroy.
The matron at Port Hedland.
The artist in Papunya.
The woman in Six Bells ...

> *Beat.*

The bells ...

Can you can hear them?

> *A large chorus of young women's recorded voices collect into an affirmation.*

VOICES: I can hear them ... I can hear them ... I hear them ... I can hear them ...

> *The* YOUNG WOMAN *looks at the audience.*

YOUNG WOMAN: Can you hear them?

> *The voices build to a cacophony. And suddenly: silence.*

THE END

www.ingramcontent.com/pod-product-compliance
Lightning Source LLC
Chambersburg PA
CBHW050027090426
42734CB00021B/3449